How To
DISCIPLINE
FLESH
YOUR

Kenneth Copeland Publications
Fort Worth, Texas

How to Discipline Your Flesh

ISBN 1-57562-116-9   30-0044

Reprinted 1996

All scripture is from the *King James Version* unless otherwise noted.

Kenneth Copeland Publications
Fort Worth, Texas 76192-0001

How to Discipline
Your Flesh

"We are more than conquerors."
That's what the Word of God says
about us as believers.

But there was a time in my life
when that victorious description
just didn't seem to apply to me. I
was born again; I had made Jesus
Christ the Lord of my life, but
something was still wrong.

Instead of living like a conqueror, I was getting conquered by

everything from sickness to ciga-rettes to coconut pie. It's not that I didn't put up a fight against those things. I did! I tried—and failed—to whip them...over...and over...and over again.

You know exactly what I'm talking about, don't you? You've been there, and you're not alone. There are believers everywhere who are caught right now in that kind of defeat. Most of them have "repented and rededicated" more times than they can remember. But every time they take a fresh stand against the devil, he just knocks them flat again.

It doesn't have to be that way.

That's what I found out more than 20 years ago and my life has never been the same since. I found out that I *could* live as "more than a conqueror." That I could fight the good fight of faith like a winner so that when the fight was done, the devil would be the one left sprawled on the mat.

You can do the same thing. No matter how many areas you may have failed in, no matter how many times those failures have been repeated, if you'll apply the truths I'm about to show you from the Word of God, you can turn those failures around. You can finally begin to live like the mighty and victorious conqueror you have been born again to be.

The Battlefield of the Mind

Before you can consistently enjoy that kind of victory, however, you must go to the Word and learn something about the strategies the devil is using against you. You must learn how he operates, so you can put a stop to those operations in your life.

You must find out, for example, exactly where he's going to attack you. After all, you can hardly expect to win the war if you can't even find your way to the battlefield.

Hebrews 12:1-3 will help turn you in the right direction. It says:

Wherefore seeing we also are compassed about with so great a cloud of witnesses, let us lay

aside every weight, and the sin which doth so easily beset us, and let us run with patience the race that is set before us, Looking unto Jesus the author and finisher of our faith; who for the joy that was set before him endured the cross, despising the shame, and is set down at the right hand of the throne of God. For consider him that endured such contradiction of sinners against himself, lest ye be wearied and faint in your minds.

Read that last phrase again. "Consider Jesus...lest ye be wearied and faint *in your minds.*"

As long as you live in a mortal body, your mind is the place where your fight with Satan will be won or lost. Your mind is the battlefield.

Some people have made the mistake of thinking Satan's attacks come in the realm of the spirit, but they don't! Jesus defeated him once and for all where the spirit realm is concerned—and when we made Jesus Lord of our lives, that victory became forever ours. The battle for your spirit is over. It has already been fought and won. As a believer, you've been spiritually reborn into the image of God, and there is absolutely nothing the devil can do to change that. He's been permanently kicked out of that domain.

Unless you understand the difference between the soul and the spirit, that may be difficult for you to grasp. So let me give you an illustration that will help you see the distinction between the two.

Over the years, I've met a few people who, through supernatural visions, have had the privilege of actually seeing Jesus. In describing their visions, several of those people have told me the same thing. They've said that when Jesus appeared to them, almost all of the questions they'd always wanted to ask Him suddenly vanished from their minds. Then later, when the vision was gone, they'd think about that great opportunity they had and wonder how on earth they could have failed to ask Him those questions when they had the chance. *Why didn't I ask Him about this?* they'd think. *Why didn't I ask Him about that?*

I'll tell you why they didn't. It was because visions take place in the realm of the spirit; and when you're operating purely in the realm of the spirit, your mind (which is in the realm of the soul) is not in charge. The only questions those folks could think to ask were questions that had truly been in their spirits. All the others—the ones they so quickly forgot—were simply questions they'd been entertaining in their minds.

When those folks were caught up in those visions, the devil wasn't even a factor. Because they had for that moment stepped totally into the spirit, he couldn't get in and mess things up. Even though he himself is a spirit, he's lost all his authority in the spiritual realm. He can't fight you there anymore. Remember, 1 Corinthians 10:13 says, *"There hath no temptation taken you but such as is common to man."* That means Satan has to operate in this natural, soulish realm. And even in this realm he has no authority, but he can try to deceive you. Deception is all that he has.

That doesn't mean, however, that he'll just pack up and go home. He's still going to come after you. He's still going to try to steal from you and kill you and destroy you—and he's going to try to do it by gaining control of your mind. By bombarding you with destructive thoughts and putting pressure on your emotions.

You need to know that. You need to prepare yourself for it. You need to realize that if you're ever going to take a successful stand against him, you're going to have to do it on the battlefield of your mind.

Defeat by Deceit

Now that you know where the fight is going to take place, you need to know what kind of weapons the devil is going to use against you.

That's not really too tough to figure out. He only has one, and I can describe it to you in one word: deceit.

He has to use deceit because he doesn't have the power to defeat you any other way. He doesn't have the power to win outright. In fact, he doesn't have *any* power of his own. Jesus stripped him of it all when He arose from the dead and took away from him the keys of hell and death.

He has to win the battle in your soul by tricking you into defeating yourself. He must somehow deceive you into setting aside the victorious life of righteousness and con you into stepping again into the slavery of sin.

"Well now, Brother Copeland," you may say, "I'm certainly not going to fall for that. I've been chairman of the deacons too long to get sucked back into a life of *sin!*"

There have been a great many believers who said that same thing and yet ended up totally shipwrecked, their lives torn apart by sins they never expected to fall into. Like you, those believers would never have jumped headlong into a life of hard-core sin. But somehow, without even realizing it, they kept inching toward it a little at a time until at last they slipped right over the edge.

You see, sin never starts out big. It begins small and grows. The devil doesn't just come blaring up to you and say, *Why don't you be a prostitute? Why don't you be a killer?*

He starts by planting a little seed in your mind. He starts by causing you to wonder, for example, what would happen if you cursed just a little bit.

Let me tell you, I'm speaking from experience when I say that because that is exactly how the devil started with me. I was raised in a Christian home. I grew up knowing that it was wrong to curse. In fact, I figured, as a little boy, that for me it might well be downright dangerous. I didn't know but what God would just strike me dead if I ever said so much as one curse word.

Of course, I knew that other people did it. I had relatives who were practically geniuses at it. I just didn't think God would put up with it out of me.

But one day when I was 9 years old, I started thinking about it. I started wondering just what would happen if I cursed. Now I don't mean I just thought about it once or twice. I thought about it for hours. I absolutely couldn't get it off my mind.

We had a long driveway back then that ran from the street to the garage behind our house, and I paced up and down that driveway all morning long, thinking about cursing the whole time. The idea of it just kept working on my mind hour after hour. I'd think, *Boy, God doesn't want me to do this. Momma doesn't want me to do this. Daddy doesn't want me to do this. But I want to do it!*

I wrestled with those thoughts way up into the afternoon. Then finally I decided. I was going to do it. *If I die, I die,* I thought. It took all the courage I had to say just about a half a word. But I did it. Nothing happened. Lightning didn't strike. I didn't drop dead. Nothing. So I finished that word and started another.

Suddenly, the dam broke. I started cursing everything in sight. I walked up and down that driveway cursing the whole time. Of course, in Texas we don't curse, we cuss! I'd kick a rock and cuss it. I cussed the dog, the cat, the house. I cussed the garage. I called that garage everything I could think of. Boy, I mean, I was getting with it.

That doesn't really sound like such a big deal, does it? A 9-year-old boy on a little cussing spree? But I'll tell you, that afternoon something moved in on my life. I knew it even then, although I wouldn't have been able to tell you just what it was. I knew something destructive had moved in on me.

From that point on, it began to take over. It literally began to rule my life. Over the years, it nearly destroyed me spiritually, mentally and physically.

You see, Satan had come and planted the seed of rebellion. It was just a little thing at first. But it grew. Pretty soon I was smoking everything I could get my hands on. At 11 years old, I'd shred cedar bark and smoke it. It didn't taste good either—felt like it set my neck on fire every time. But I did it anyway because something was inside me pushing me to do it.

By the time I was a grown man, I was rebellious to everything that had a legal tone to it. I was rebellious to the law. I was rebellious to my mother and father. I was rebellious to God. On the one hand, I wanted God. But on the other hand, I didn't because I didn't want to do what He told me to do. I thought that if I threw off those kinds of restraints, I could be free. But the truth was, I was in bondage the whole time.

My flesh—my natural, human appetites and desires—became the boss of everything I did. By receiving that seed of rebellion, I'd set a law in motion and I didn't know how to stop it. By the time I was 20 years old, I was 100 pounds overweight, smoking over a pack and a half of cigarettes a day—rebellious, self-seeking and mad at everybody who loved me. I knew I was headed for destruction, but I couldn't stop it. I was out of control. My body was out of control, and I didn't know how to put on the brakes.

Then, when I finally made Jesus Lord of my life and got delivered from all that, I found I couldn't *stay* delivered. The Lord would set me free all right. But then Satan would come right in behind, planting those little seeds in my mind. They'd start to grow and then I'd find myself right back in bondage again.

As a born-again believer, I certainly had the power to be an overcomer. But because I didn't understand the strategy of the devil, I kept being overcome!

Eventually, though, after searching the Word and seeking answers from the Lord, I began to get wise to that strategy—and I found a way to counter it. It's a way so simple, you can teach it to a child. Yet it is so full of power, it can literally set you free in any area of your life.

Lasciviousness:
The First Point of Attack

To help you begin to understand how this strategy works, I want to draw your attention to a peculiar word found in the New Testament. It's probably not a word you've heard very often. In fact, it took me a long time just to learn how to say it, much less find out what it meant. But it's a crucial part of the devil's battle plan, and you need to learn something about it.

The word is "lasciviousness." Some translations call it "licentiousness" and, scripturally speaking, it keeps very bad company. In Mark 7:20-23, for example, Jesus includes it along with adultery, fornication, murder, (and a number of other sins) as one of the things that defile a man. In Galatians 5, it's listed between "uncleanness" and "idolatry" as one of the works of the flesh.

The actual meaning of lasciviousness is "no restraint or

unrestrained"; and the reason I believe it's such an important word is that it's the devil's first and most important point of attack on the life of a believer. If he can conquer you there, he's got it made.

You see, he knows that if you're going to live a godly life, you'll have to restrain the desires and appetites of your flesh. You'll have to put your spirit in charge and make your flesh yield to and come under the authority of the Holy Spirit within you.

Satan's goal, of course, is to stop you from doing that. So, through lasciviousness, he starts applying pressure to your flesh, causing its appetites to grow stronger. He starts trying to talk you into letting go of your restraint here and there. Not much at first, of course. Just a little now and again. Until suddenly, almost before you know it, your flesh begins to take control. It starts dominating your spirit.

You find yourself doing things you really don't want to do. Giving in to the weaknesses of your flesh. If food is your greatest weakness, for example, that's where the cycle will begin. Food is the physical ground for more human failure and lasciviousness than any other item. Satan used it to successfully tempt Adam and Eve. Then he tried to use it again against Jesus by coming to Him when He was hungry and telling Him to turn stones into bread.

The desire for food is a powerful, powerful thing. But if you'll get some insight into lasciviousness and refuse to let that desire control you, many of you can start right now and get rid of about two-thirds of that fat you've been carrying around. That's what happened to me. I got rid of about 100 pounds of my body weight. But I didn't do it by just going on a diet. I had to stop lasciviousness in my life and the weight took care of itself.

Regardless of whether your weakness is for food or something else, however, the signs of lasciviousness are always the same. Little by little, you find yourself starting to lose control. Eating too much.

Eating things you know not to eat. drinking too much. Gossiping now and then. Inside, you're miserable. *Oh my, I need to stop this,* you think. But somehow you just can't seem to do it. The restraints have been removed and your flesh has taken charge.

That's how lasciviousness works, and though it gets far less publicity than things like adultery and murder, in the end it is just as devastating.

The truth is, all sin is the same. The devil has just packaged it in different ways. Sexual sins have one kind of ribbon around them. Gluttony has another kind of ribbon around it. But take off the wrapping and it all comes down to the same thing—and that's selfishness.

You don't eat that extra piece of pie for somebody else's benefit, do you? You don't cheat on your taxes to help others, do you? No, You do it for your own sweet self. You don't commit adultery for someone else either. Every sin begins the same way. It begins when the big "ME" becomes predominant in your thinking either through fear or through pride or through a combination of the two.

Just as all sins have a common beginning, they also have a common end—and in Ephesians 4, we can see exactly what that end is. So let's take a look, beginning with verse 17:

This I say therefore, and testify in the Lord, that ye henceforth walk not as other Gentiles walk, in the vanity of their mind, Having the understanding darkened, being alienated from the life of God through the ignorance that is in them, because of the blindness of their heart: Who being past feeling [or dead to shame, having the conscience seared until it has no more voice to the mind or the body] have given themselves over unto lasciviousness, to work all uncleanness with greediness.

What we see there in that passage is the progression of sin. It begins when you allow yourself to be controlled by the thoughts

Satan plants in your mind. Then it keeps on pushing you further and further until you are totally given over to it—read that last phrase again—"working ALL uncleanness with greediness."

Think about that. ALL uncleanness! The ultimate goal of Satan is to use lasciviousness to bring you again into total slavery to sin. His plan is to pressure you into yielding to the weakness of your flesh until that weakness begins to dominate you.

If he can do that, he can defeat you. He can see to it that you end up living a life of failure. He can make you live just like the unsaved people of the world have to live—despite the fact that you're a born-again, Holy Spirit-baptized child of God.

I don't care if you're the most anointed pastor who ever lived. I don't care if you've been chairman of the deacons for 25 years. If you start giving up your restraint and giving into the desires of your flesh, through lasciviousness Satan can bring you to a place where you're living like an unbeliever. Living a life alienated from the life of God. Working all uncleanness, with greediness. He can bring you to a place where you have no shame about you at all.

That's a terrible, terrible end. It is an end marked by big sins.

But always remember, every one of those "big sins" had small beginnings.

It Starts With a Thought

Now let's zero in and look at Satan's strategy even closer. Let's break it down and examine it step by step and see exactly how it works.

We've already established the fact that Satan is not going to begin by trying to totally wipe out every trace of God in your life. He's not going to waltz in and suggest, right off the bat, that you fly to Las Vegas and blow $8,000 gambling. He's not going to start pushing you toward adultery the first day.

He's much more subtle than that. He begins by planting a thought in your mind. A simple thought. No big deal, really. Oh yes, it's a thought you know you shouldn't be entertaining but...it seems harmless enough at the time.

Let's say, for example, that some-one at work treats you unfairly. You know you should forgive him and forget it, but instead you begin to go over the incident again and again in your mind. A little bitter-ness sprouts up. *I know I shouldn't be thinking like this,* you say to yourself, *but I just can't help it. After all, that guy had no right to treat me that way.*

Instead of restraining that thought, you just let it go. *After all, how much harm could one little thought do?* you think, and you allow Satan to deceive you into believing such thoughts are too small and insignificant to bother with.

All the while, however, he knows he's planting the seeds of your destruction one little thought at a time.

Then, almost before you know what's happening, somebody walks into the room and your mouth flies open and you start saying ugly things about that person at the office. You start gossiping. You're thinking all the while, *I need to stop this. I need to quit saying these unloving things.* But you don't stop. You failed to restrain your thoughts and now you're unable to restrain your tongue.

Don't fool yourself by thinking you can talk ugly about somebody and then act loving toward them either. You can't. Your actions are going to fall right in line with your words. That's a biblical principle.

The book of James tells us bluntly that if any man can control his tongue, he can control his whole body. Your tongue is the rudder of your life. It determines your course; and no matter how hard you try to stop it, it's eventually going to start repeating those thoughts you've been entertaining in your mind.

One of the most deadly results of unrestrained thinking is doubt.

That's right! Doubt is a direct result of lasciviousness. Doubt comes when you allow yourself to indulge in thoughts that are contrary to the Word of God.

Instead of thinking about what the Word says concerning your health, for example, you allow yourself to start thinking about sickness. *I know the Bible says "By His stripes I am healed," but I'll tell you what, I sure don't feel healed. My back hurts and my head hurts and I'm just sure I'm catching the flu. How could I be healed when I feel this bad?*

It's not that you mean to be rebelling against the Word. It's just that you fail to restrain the thoughts that are contrary to it. You simply allow them to flow through your mind, and before you know it, they've crippled your faith and made it feeble.

That's when Satan moves in on you with sickness and disease. He lets you rob yourself of the faith power it would take for you to run him off. Then he hits you with something bigger, knowing full well that you've been so weakened by those unrestrained thoughts of doubt and unbelief that you'll be completely unable to withstand his attack.

It's a deadly sequence and it works the same way every time. Satan plants the thought—which gives birth to the words—which gives birth to the actions and events around you. Unrestrained thoughts lead inevitably to unrestrained words which lean inevitably to an unrestrained life—and an unrestrained life is doomed to destruction.

Countering the Attack

How do you keep from falling prey to the devil's plan and slipping into that dangerous sequence?

You'll find that information in 2 Corinthians 10:3-5.

For though we walk in the flesh, we do not war after the flesh: (For the weapons of our warfare are not carnal, but

mighty through God to the pulling down of strongholds;) Casting down imaginations, and every high thing that exalteth itself against the knowledge of God, and bringing into captivity every thought to the obedience of Christ.

As you keep that scripture in mind, let me ask you something. In John 1, who did the Apostle John say that Jesus was? He said He was the Word of God made flesh (John 1:14). Jesus *is* the Word of God.

In the light of that, let's read that last verse again: "Casting down imaginations, and every high thing that exalteth itself against the knowledge of God and

BRING INTO CAPTIVITY EVERY
THOUGHT TO THE OBEDIENCE
OF THE WORD."

If you'll catch hold of the impor-
tance of that one statement, you
can turn your life around—starting
today! You can foul up the devil's
whole strategy by taking charge of
your thoughts and bringing them
in line with the Word of God.

"But Brother Copeland," you
may say, "I thought I'd pretty well
done that. After all, I was saved
when I was 9 years old and I've
believed God's Word ever since."

No, if you're like most believers,
you really haven't. You've just believed *at* it from a distance. You've
just assented to it mentally. You're

like the person who says he believes airplanes can fly and then refuses to get on one. You believe the Bible will work, but when the pressure is on, you don't really believe it will work *for you.*

As long as you have that attitude, you will not be able to bring every thought into captivity to the Word. If your bank account starts getting low, you'll start to worry. Then you'll think, *Well, you know the Word says that God will supply all my needs. So, maybe I should just trust Him and go on.*

Then the devil will put in his two cents worth and say something like, *But you don't know for sure if you can count on that. After all,*

Uncle Charlie is one of those faith nuts, and he went bankrupt last year. Before you know it, you have let those money worries come right back. You'll quit restraining them and just let them romp around in your mind, tearing up what little bit of faith you had.

So, the first thing you must do to counter the devil's attack is make a quality decision (that's a decision from which there is no turning back!) that you're going to believe the Word of God. Not from a distance, but up close. As if your name were written in front of every verse.

That in itself will take you a long way toward victory. However, it won't get you all the way there. If you want to be the champion on the battlefield of your mind, you must literally reprogram it with the Word of God. Let me show you why.

Do you remember what I said earlier about your spirit being recreated in the image of God at the moment you made Jesus Lord of your life? Well, that's true. It was. At that instant, every trace of sin and every mark it had made on your spirit was totally washed away. You literally became a new creature.

Your mind, however, remained the same. The memories and thought patterns within it that had been twisted and warped by years of darkness and sin were left perfectly intact. In other words, that brand-new spirit within you suddenly found itself trying to work with a mind that had been totally programmed by the world!

As any new believer can tell you, that's an uncomfortable—and sometimes downright distressing—situation to be caught in! For, as Galatians 5:17 says, "The desires of the flesh are opposed to the spirit, and the [desires of the] spirit are opposed to the flesh; for these are antagonistic to each other—continually withstanding and in conflict with each other—so that you are not free but are prevented from doing what you desire to do," *(The Amplified Bible)*.

How do you get out of that dilemma?

By renewing your mind with the Word of God. Romans 12:2 puts it this way. *"Be not conformed to this world: but be ye transformed by the renewing of your mind...."*

Now, I want to show you something exciting, something too few believers really understand. Look back at that scripture I just quoted. Notice that it doesn't say to "retrain" your mind. It says "renew" it. Most Christians treat the Word of God like a textbook full of information. They use it to teach from and to refer to. But the Word is far, far more than that.

Hebrews 4:12 says it is "quick." That means "alive" in King James English. When you start putting the Word in your mind, you're actually putting the power of God to work in your mind. You're not just supplying it with additional information, you're bringing it under the influence of a living force, a force that will make it qualitatively different, a force that will make it *new*.

You need to understand, though, that renewing your mind is not something you can do overnight. It's something that must be done day after day and moment by moment. If you're really going to bring every thought into captivity to the obedience of the word, you must start your day with the Word of God—and you're going to have to keep that Word flowing in at every opportunity.

If you will do that, you'll be absolutely amazed at what the Word can do. I remember the first time I discovered that. I was attending a Charles Rogers meeting in Rev. Hilton Sutton's church in Houston, Texas. I'd been saved a couple of years, but I was still in tremendous bondage and I was absolutely miserable!

I knew I was supposed to be in the ministry, but I couldn't figure out how. I'd tell God that I'd do anything He wanted me to do. But then when He began giving me specific instructions, I'd argue with Him. "Oh no, Lord," I'd say. "I couldn't possibly do that. I'd go broke!" Because I failed to restrain those kinds of thoughts, lasciviousness would step in and I'd start going downhill again.

Now here's something I want you to notice. (I'll get back to Brother Sutton's church in a moment.) Lasciviousness works two ways. On the one hand, it causes your flesh to be *unrestrained,* but at the same time, it causes you to *restrain* the godly promptings of your spirit! Lasciviousness lets your flesh run wild while putting your spirit in bondage. It prevents you from following the leadership of the Holy Spirit.

Lasciviousness just had me tied up in knots when I went to Houston. In addition to keeping me from the ministry, it had also kept me addicted to tobacco. I can't tell you how many times I tried to get free of the habit. I'd throw a pack of cigarettes out the car window and then turn around and go back and get them. I'd feel like a fool walking around out there in a ditch hunting for those cigarettes I'd just thrown out.

Sometimes I'd want to be rid of them so badly that I'd run over them. Then I'd get crying mad about it because I didn't have money enough to buy any more. I'd stand there and almost cry over something that was killing me!

That's what lasciviousness will do for you. It will turn you into a fool.

When I got to Houston, I put a pack of cigarettes up over the sun visor in my car and left them there. I knew I was going to be around preachers the whole time I was there and I didn't want to smoke around them, not because they would chew me out about it, but because I respected them. (They were far too loving to jump on me about anything. They might shove me in a corner and pray for me all night long, but they wouldn't chew me out.)

For a few hours, I had a reason not to smoke that was more powerful than my desire to smoke—and my reason was my respect for these men of God. Of course, if that had been all there was to it, it wouldn't have lasted for long. Lasciviousness is more powerful than that.

You may put away your tobacco because you have respect for your wife and she hates the filthy stuff. You may quit for a while because you don't want your children to do it. But under the pressure of the devil, that reason will soon wear thin, and eventually you'll do it again. You'll start out smoking where they can't see you. Sneaking around and lying about it. But finally you'll get mad and say, "Who are they to tell me when I can smoke and when I can't!" Then you'll be hooked all over again.

But, praise God, something more powerful than lasciviousness got hold of me there in Houston. The Word! I just went to one meeting right after another and listened to the Word being preached. I got totally caught up in it. I didn't want to go anywhere else. I didn't want to do anything else. I just wanted to be in there where the Word was going forth.

In several services, Brother Sutton preached on the second coming of Jesus. I got so high on it, I could hardly sit still. In between the meetings, I'd hang around him and Brother Rogers and the other preachers. I stayed at their heels all the time. When they had conversations about the Word and about faith, I'd just butt in and start asking questions.

You see, I'd wormed my way in there by offering to sing for them. Then I milked that opportunity for all it was worth. Every time they had a meal, they had to drag me along. I went everywhere they went. I wanted to hear everything they had to say.

One afternoon, for example, I heard Hilton Sutton say, "You know, a man is healed before he can see it." I thought, *What does that mean? How could you be healed before you see it?* That bothered me all afternoon. Instead of thinking about cigarettes, I spent all my time wondering how you can be healed before you see it.

For over 2 1/2 weeks, I was surrounded by the Word of God. I was completely absorbed in it. Then when I got back into my car to go home, I saw those cigarettes. They were still there over the sun visor, right where I'd left them. I hadn't even thought about them for almost three weeks.

Do you see what happened? The Word had gotten inside me and begun to work. It had wiped that addiction right out of my mind. By the time I left those meetings, I didn't have any desire to smoke, and it wasn't until I saw those cigarettes sitting up there that I realized it.

Man alive! I thought. *I've been three weeks without those things. I might as well not pick them up now.* I started to throw them away, but then I thought, *No, I'm just going to leave them there. Praise God, I'm either delivered or I'm not.* So that's where they stayed. Eventually, they dried up so much the tobacco dropped down in my face while I was driving. So I threw them away and that was the end of that.

What I discovered in those meetings changed my life. I discovered that if I would put the Word of God in my mind and keep it there, it would set me free. It would give me victory.

Over the years, I've continued to find out just how powerful the

Word is. I've seen it change my mind and my body and my circumstances. You know, Hebrews 5:14 says that through practice the flesh can be trained to know the difference between good and evil, and I've seen that happen in my own life.

My flesh has been so thoroughly Word-trained in some areas that the devil can't get to first base there. If, for example, he ever approaches me with any thought of being unfaithful to my wife, I nail him instantly. I don't sit around and say, "Oh now, I ought not be thinking that way."

No sir. My mind has been so renewed by the Word of God and

that Word has given me such a revelation of love for her that my very flesh recoils immediately from the thought. Before I even think, a fury rises up inside me and just slaps that filthy thing down.

That's how powerfully the Word of God can affect you.

Once you understand that, I guarantee you, you'll go out of your way not only to read and study the Word but to get to meetings where it's being preached as well. You'll begin to see why such meetings are so important.

Most people don't have any grasp of that at all. God will send a faith-filled preacher of the Word to their town and spend hundreds of thousands of dollars to rent the convention center to make it possible for them to come and sit and just soak up the Word for days. All the people would have to do to reprogram their consciousness with power and with the Word of God would be to come, sit and listen. When those meetings are over, they could walk out, leaving their sin and defeat behind them. They could go home with great faith and victory instead.

But instead of beating a path to that convention center day and night, they give excuses about why they can't come. "Well, I'd like to be there, but I've got a Little League game tonight," they say. Or "I have to cook some pies for the bake sale at church." My friend, somewhere down the line, all of us are going to have to answer for all that. We're going to have to try and explain why we were too busy for the Word of God, and we're not going to be able to do it. We have no excuse.

Looking to Jesus

Now that you've begun to see just how vital the Word is to your victory, let's look again at the instructions we saw earlier in Hebrews 12:

Wherefore seeing we also are compassed about with so great a cloud of witnesses, let us lay aside every weight, and

**the sin which doth so easily
beset us, and let us run with
patience the race that is set
before us, Looking unto Jesus
the author and finisher of our
faith...(verses 1-2).**

There are many, many believers
today who are struggling with all
their might to lay aside the sins
that defeat them. However, most of
them are failing miserably. Why?
These are not bad people. Quite
the contrary. They are sincere people who love God but—because
they've missed an important part
of the message that passage con-
veys, they are still in bondage.

You see, it doesn't just say, "...Lay
aside the sin." It doesn't just say,
"You shape up and be holy!" It

says, "Look at Jesus!" Get rid of the sin by looking at Jesus!

Everyone wants to do that but most people don't have any idea how it's done. The only way they know to see Jesus (or anyone else for that matter) is with their natural eyes. I used to think like that too. During my first five years as a Christian, I wanted to see Him so badly I could hardly stand it. I wanted Him to appear to me in a vision or something. I thought if He would ever do that, I'd be able to get rid of all the junk that had been bothering me.

I finally saw Him all right, but not like I'd expected. I saw Him in the Word. I've been seeing Him in the

Word now for well over 20 years, and I'm telling you, I know what He is like. I know His nature. I know Him better than I know anybody. I don't know Him yet as well as I want to, but thanks to the Word I know Him better continually.

I now know how to bring my thoughts into obedience to Him because I know Him with all my heart. People believed for years they were bringing their thoughts into obedience to Jesus by thinking things like, *God put cancer on man to teach him something.* But they did not know Jesus. Had they seen Him in the Word, they would never have dared think such a thing.

Sometimes people try to know God through their emotions. They go to church meetings and get stirred up emotionally, saying, "Oh, don't we feel God!" Are you kidding? We can't even begin to know God through our emotions or our physical senses. We should be emotional about the things of God. There's nothing wrong with that. We can have momentary rushes of feeling. But those feelings won't last five minutes when the storms of life hit. We need something far more trustworthy than that.

If we're going to live out the victory God has given us through the Cross, we must do it with the Word of God hidden in our hearts, alive in our brains, and flowing out our mouths. The Word must be first place in our lives, to believe it and act on it even when (especially when) all hell breaks loose around us.

Does that sound like a tall order?

I won't kid you, it is. This is something you'll have to work at, my friend. You'll have to work at it every day. You can't be spiritually lazy and walk off this battlefield a champion.

If you want to be a winner, you'll have to set your mind and your heart on the Word of God above all else. You'll have to make a firm decision to take authority over every thought that comes into your mind. You must decide once and for all that you will, with the

Holy Spirit's help, learn enough about Jesus in His Word to bring your thoughts into obedience to Him.

The choice is yours. Will you continue to drag yourself from one defeat to another, to roll over and play dead on the battlefield of life? Or will you make the quality decision to be what Jesus went to the cross to produce: the most powerful being this side of heaven?

From here on out, it's really up to you.

Prayer for Salvation and Baptism in the Holy Spirit

Heavenly Father, I come to You in the Name of Jesus. Your Word says, *"...whosoever shall call on the name of the Lord shall be saved"* (Acts 2:21). I am calling on You. I pray and ask Jesus to come into my heart and be Lord over my life according to Romans 10:9-10. *"If thou shalt confess with thy mouth the Lord Jesus, and shalt believe in thine heart that God hath raised him from the dead, thou shalt be saved."* I do that now. I confess that Jesus is Lord, and I believe in my heart that God raised Him from the dead.

I am now reborn! I am a Christian— a child of Almighty God! I am saved! You also said in Your Word, *"If ye then, being evil, know how to give good gifts unto your children: HOW MUCH MORE shall your heavenly Father give the Holy Spirit to them that ask him?"* (Luke 11:13).

I'm also asking You to fill me with the Holy Spirit. Holy Spirit, rise up within me as I praise God. I fully expect to speak with other tongues as You give me the utterance (Acts 2:4).

Begin to praise God for filling you with the Holy Spirit. Speak those words and syllables you receive—not in your own language, but the language given to you by the Holy Spirit. You have to use your own voice. God will not force you to speak.

Now you are a Spirit-filled believer. Continue with the blessing God has given you and pray in tongues each day. You'll never be the same!

Find a good Word of God preaching church, and become a part of a church family who will love and care for you as you love and care for them.

We need to be hooked up to each other. It increases our strength in God. It's God's plan for us.

Books by Kenneth Copeland

*Available in Spanish

Books by Gloria Copeland

*   And Jesus Healed Them All
Are You Ready?
Build Yourself an Ark
From Faith to Faith—A Daily Guide to Victory
God's Prescription for Divine Health
God's Success Formula
God's Will for You
God's Will for Your Healing
God's Will Is Prosperity
God's Will Is the Holy Spirit
*   Harvest of Health
Healing Promises
Love—The Secret to Your Success
No Deposit—No Return
Pressing In—It's Worth It All
The Power to Live a New Life
The Unbeatable Spirit of Faith
*   Walk in the Spirit
Walk With God
Well Worth the Wait

*Available in Spanish

Other Books Published by KCP

Heirs Together by Mac Hammond
John G. Lake—His Life, His Sermons,
   His Boldness of Faith
Winning the World by Mac Hammond

World Offices
of Kenneth Copeland Ministries

For more information about KCM and a free catalog, please write the office nearest you:

Kenneth Copeland Ministries
Fort Worth, Texas 76192-0001

Kenneth Copeland
Locked Bag 2600
Mansfield Delivery Centre
QUEENSLAND 4122
AUSTRALIA

Kenneth Copeland
Post Office Box 15
BATH
BA1 1GD
ENGLAND

Kenneth Copeland
Post Office Box 830
RANDBURG
2125
REPUBLIC OF SOUTH AFRICA

Kenneth Copeland
Post Office Box 58248
Vancouver
BRITISH COLUMBIA
V6P 6K1
CANADA

220123 MINSK
REPUBLIC OF BELARUS
Post Office 123
P/B 35
Kenneth Copeland Ministries